CONTENTS

Robert Winter   Christopher Wright   Iohn Wright   Thomas Percy   Guido Fawkes   Robert Catesby   Thomas Winter

■ REMEMBER, REMEMBER! ■

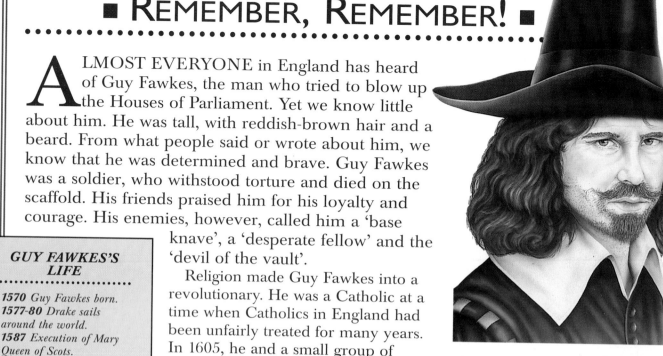

ALMOST EVERYONE in England has heard of Guy Fawkes, the man who tried to blow up the Houses of Parliament. Yet we know little about him. He was tall, with reddish-brown hair and a beard. From what people said or wrote about him, we know that he was determined and brave. Guy Fawkes was a soldier, who withstood torture and died on the scaffold. His friends praised him for his loyalty and courage. His enemies, however, called him a 'base knave', a 'desperate fellow' and the 'devil of the vault'.

Religion made Guy Fawkes into a revolutionary. He was a Catholic at a time when Catholics in England had been unfairly treated for many years. In 1605, he and a small group of fellow Catholics planned the Gunpowder Plot to get rid of England's new Protestant king, James I. By blowing up parliament when James was there, Guy Fawkes and his friends hoped to start a rebellion that would make England a Catholic country once more.

The plot failed. The day of its discovery and Guy Fawkes's arrest, 5 November, was made a day of public thanksgiving by parliament. Ever since, the fate of Guy Fawkes has been celebrated with bonfires and fireworks on that day. 'Remember, remember, the Fifth of November, gunpowder, treason and plot . . .'

GUY FAWKES'S LIFE

1570 Guy Fawkes born.
1577-80 Drake sails around the world.
1587 Execution of Mary Queen of Scots.
1588 Spanish Armada.
1601 Earl of Essex leads a rebellion.
1603 Queen Elizabeth I dies. James VI of Scotland becomes James I of England.
1604 Guy Fawkes joins plot to kill James.
1605 Gunpowder Plot discovered.
1606 Guy Fawkes executed.

▲ Guy Fawkes – a brave soldier who turned his talents to treachery and plotted to deal a deadly 'blow'.

▶ Guy Fawkes entering parliament. This print, made soon after the event, shows the 'hand of God' pointing accusingly from a cloud at the 'deed of darkness'.

▼ Children collecting 'pennies for the guy'. This 19th-century illustration shows them wheeling a stuffed guy through the streets.

▼ Guy Fawkes's signature, after torture.

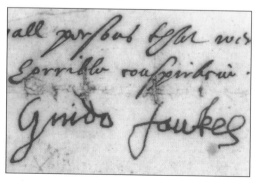

■ ENGLAND DIVIDED ■

G UY FAWKES WAS born in the England of Queen Elizabeth I. The date of his birth is not known, but he was baptized on 16 April 1570 in the church of St Michael le Belfrey, in the ancient city of York. He was probably born three days earlier in his parents' house in Stonegate. In Tudor England, most babies were baptized at the age of three days – some did not live much longer, dying from one of the many childhood diseases that we now have medicines to cure.

HIS PARENTS

Guy's parents were Edward Fawkes, a lawyer, and his wife Edith. Guy's mother came from a family called Jackson that had Catholic sympathies. Her sister's son (Guy's cousin) became a Jesuit priest. But Edward Fawkes was a Protestant. To keep his job, he had to swear an oath of loyalty to the queen. England's queen, like her father Henry VIII, was head of the Church in England. It was Henry who had begun England's quarrel with the Catholic Church in Rome.

▲ The Catholic Mary Tudor was succeeded as queen in 1558 by her Protestant half-sister Elizabeth (bel

EVENTS

1568 Protestant Dutch rebel against rule by Catholic Spain.
1570 Guy Fawkes is born in York. Queen Elizabeth is excommunicated (expelled from the Catholic Church) by the pope, who tells Catholics it is now right and just to remove her.
1571 The Ridolfi plot to murder Elizabeth I and put the imprisoned Mary Queen of Scots on the throne is foiled. In the Mediterranean, a European fleet defeats the Turkish navy at the battle of Lepanto.
1572 Many Protestants are killed in France, in the St Bartholomew's Day Massacre.
1573 Francis Drake returns from Panama with Spanish gold.

CATHOLICS AND PROTESTANTS

Christians in Europe had been quarrelling ever since the Reformation began in the early 1500s. The Reformation was a movement to put right what was wrong in the Catholic Church, and it had split Europe. Before it, there was just one church in western Europe led by the pope in Rome. Now there were Protestant churches, too, with their own priests and ways of worship.

Elizabeth had been queen for 12 years when Guy Fawkes was born. The queen was a Protestant, but her kingdom was divided. Some people were Catholics; others were Protestants. England's chief enemy abroad was Spain, and Spain was Europe's strongest Catholic power. Protestants accused Catholics of being on the side of Spain. Into this atmosphere of fear and distrust, Guy Fawkes was born.

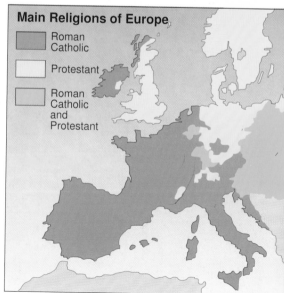

Main Religions of Europe

Roman Catholic

Protestant

Roman Catholic and Protestant

DYING FOR THEIR FAITH

ELIZABETH'S father, Henry VIII, had made himself head of the Church of England. In 1553, his daughter Mary I became queen. She was a Catholic, and married the king of Spain. Mary died in 1558, without children, and her half-sister Elizabeth became queen. Elizabeth I was a Protestant.

While Mary was queen, Protestants in England had been ill-treated. Some were burned to death for their beliefs. Under Elizabeth, it was the turn of the Catholics to suffer. The Catholic mass (church service) was forbidden and people were fined if they did not attend Protestant services. Catholics who defied the law faced imprisonment or even death.

▲ On 24 August 1572, some 20,000 Huguenots (Protestants) were killed in France during the St Bartholomew's Day Massacre.

▼ English Protestants face the gallows at Smithfield, London, during the reign of Mary Tudor.

■ BOYHOOD IN YORK ■

YORK WAS A busy cathedral city of merchants and scholars. The archbishop of York was the second most important churchman in England after the archbishop of Canterbury. Yorkshire and neighbouring Lancashire were both counties where there were many Catholics. Some were open 'recusants', people who refused to pretend to be Protestants and were on the government's blacklist as possible troublemakers.

HOME LIFE

Edward Fawkes was no troublemaker. He carried on his legal business, while his wife Edith ran the household with the help of a maidservant. The Fawkes family was comfortably off, though not wealthy. Guy's parents slept in a large wooden bed, one of their prized possessions. He slept on straw, as most children did in those days.

SCHOOLDAYS AND A HARSH LESSON

When he was five, Guy went to school for the first time. Every morning at six

▲ Lord Cobham and his family were 'recusants'. They risked losing their wealth, position and freedom by openly holding Catholic services

▼ One of the gates to the city of York, where Guy Fawkes was born and first went to school.

o'clock, he was woken by the maidservant. Gobbling a breakfast of bread and ale, he walked to St Peter's School. There he worked at his books of English grammar and Latin. He made friends with Jack and Kit Wright, two boys who were more keen on sword-fighting than study.

Religion played an important part in school life. Guy's headmaster was one of those northern Protestants who were secretly Catholic. He kept his job by telling the authorities about a local Catholic priest (who was then arrested), but he let teachers in his school tell the boys about Catholic ideas. Three of Guy's schoolfellows later became Catholic priests.

A NEW HOME

When Guy was eight, his father died. Two years later, his mother married a country gentleman named Denis Bainbridge. She and Guy's two sisters, Anne and Elizabeth, moved to Scotton, a village some miles away from York. Guy lived at school as a boarder but he went to his new home in the holidays. Bainbridge was another secret Catholic. Soon Guy was as devout a Catholic as his stepfather.

PRIEST HOLES

IT WAS A crime to say or hear the Catholic mass. Catholic priests who were caught faced gaol, torture or hanging. Many priests went into hiding and were sheltered by wealthy Catholics in their houses. Secret 'priest holes' can still be found in some old houses today. These were cramped cubbyholes with secret doors in which priests hid if the house was searched by government 'priest-hunters'. At Baddesley Clinton Hall, Warwickshire (below), the moat and sewers and secret turret trap-doors were used to conceal numerous hiding-places.

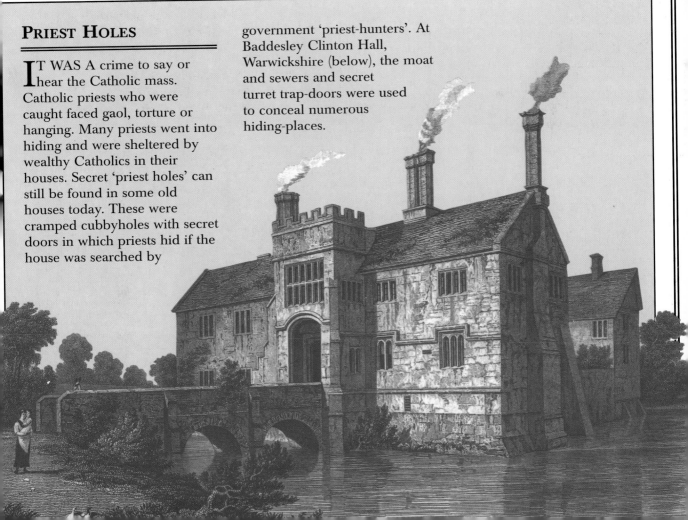

■ IN SEARCH OF ADVENTURE ■

IN 1587, MARY Stuart, Queen of Scots, was beheaded. Mary had for years been seen as a threat to Queen Elizabeth. She was a Catholic, and as granddaughter of Henry VIII's sister, had a claim to the throne of England – if Elizabeth died without children of her own. As a result, Mary had been kept prisoner in England since fleeing there from Scotland in 1568. Even so, she was still blamed for every 'Catholic' plot against Elizabeth. In the end, being part of such plots cost her her life.

FEARS OF INVASION

A year after Mary's death, Guy Fawkes left school. For a time he worked on the family farm, but country life seemed dull. He was 18 and wanted adventure.

It was 1588, the year

of the Spanish Armada. Warning beacons across the south of England stood ready to be lit in the event of an invasion. News of sea battles in the Channel came slowly to Yorkshire. The Spanish fleet had been driven away. No Catholic army had landed to remove Queen Elizabeth and replace her with a Catholic monarch. The great galleons of Spain were blown north by gales to perish on the rocky coasts of Scotland and Ireland.

A MARRIED MAN?

Not much is known about Guy's life at this time. One story tells that he married when he was 19 or so, and had a son. But there is no proof or later mention of a family. Possibly both his wife and baby died at or soon after the birth.

We do know that he left home. He travelled south to Sussex, to join the household of a Catholic nobleman named Viscount Montague as a gentleman-attendant. But he did not stay long.

▲ The execution of Mary Queen of Scots at Fotheringhay Castle.

◀ The Browne brothers; members of the family who employed Guy Fawkes.

SPAIN'S INVASION FAILS

IN 1588 THE Spanish sent a fleet of 130 ships – the Armada (below) – to attack England in retaliation for English support for Protestant rebels in the Netherlands, the execution of Mary Queen of Scots, and raids on Spanish shipping. The plan was to defeat the English navy, so that a Spanish army could cross the Channel and invade England. English Catholics had told the king of Spain that such an invasion would be welcomed by many English people. During July and August 1588, the Spanish battled their way up the Channel, fighting off the English fleet led by commanders Howard, Drake (right), Hawkins and Frobisher. They failed to join forces with Spanish troops in the Netherlands and were driven northwards around the British Isles by storms. Only half the Spanish ships got home and 15,000 soldiers and sailors perished.

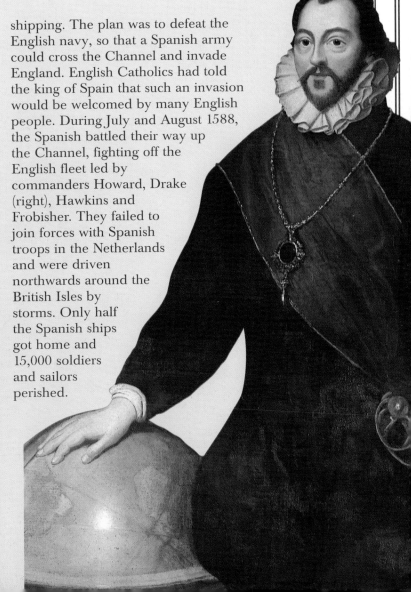

■ A SOLDIER ABROAD ■

WITH MONEY TO buy a horse and clothes, and a letter of introduction from his Catholic friends, Guy Fawkes set off across the Channel. He sailed to the Spanish Netherlands (now Holland and Belgium), where he offered to fight for Spain. Many foreign soldiers were paid by Spain to fight against the Protestant Dutch rebels. Guy did not care that the Dutch were fighting for their freedom. By fighting for Spain, he believed he was defending the Catholic Church.

CHOOSING SIDES

Some time after his arrival, Guy joined Sir William Stanley's regiment. Stanley was an experienced soldier, who had fought for years in the Netherlands. At first, he had fought in an English army supporting the Dutch rebels. Then he changed sides and was now fighting for Spain. The English government had added Stanley to its list of traitors.

THE DUTCH REVOLT

SPAIN HAD ruled the Netherlands since 1519, but a revolt inspired by Dutch Protestants broke out in 1568. Resistance by rebels, including those fighting the Duke of Alba at Haarlem in 1578 (above), weakened Spain's hold, and in

EVENTS

1592 Clement VIII becomes pope.
1593 English playwright (and possible secret agent) Christopher Marlowe is killed in a brawl at an inn at Deptford. The Protestant king Henry IV of France becomes a Roman Catholic, saying 'Paris is worth a mass'.
1595 Walter Raleigh explores the Orinoco River in South America seeking gold.
1595 Shakespeare writes A Midsummer Night's Dream.
1596 Francis Drake dies on a raid in the Caribbean.
1598 King Philip II of Spain dies. End of religious wars in France.
1599 The Globe theatre opens in London.
1600 Battle of Nieuwpoort won by Dutch. East India Company founded for trade with Asia.

◀ Sir William Stanley abandoned the Dutch cause to fight for Spain – with Guy Fawkes in his regiment.

▲ A town under siege. Attackers tried to blast their way in through the walls, using gunpowder.

ERLEM.

581 the Dutch declared
ndependence. Their leader was
William the Silent, prince of
Orange. William believed in
reedom of religion, and was
nourned as a Protestant hero
fter he was assassinated by a
Catholic in 1584. The war
etween the Dutch and
panish continued off and
n until 1648 when Spain
nally recognized Dutch
ndependence.

Anyone who served with him was also a traitor. Guy
Fawkes had chosen sides.

GUNPOWDER EXPERT

The young red-headed Yorkshireman soon won a name for
bravery. He became a 'sapper', digging tunnels under the
walls of enemy towns and blowing them sky-high with
barrels of gunpowder. Handling gunpowder was tricky, but
Guy Fawkes showed great coolness. Stanley said he should
be made a captain. He was a person who could be trusted
to do what he was told, and do it well.

There were others like Guy, soldiering abroad. One was
Thomas Wintour, who at first fought for the Protestants,
even though his uncle, a Catholic priest, had been hanged.
Like Stanley, Wintour changed sides. He became a
Catholic, and he and Guy Fawkes were to meet again.

▼ William the Silent's son
and successor, Prince
Maurice of Orange-Nassau,
arrives triumphant in
Rotterdam in 1600 after
the battle of Nieuwpoort,
in which the Spaniards
were beaten.

■ DEATH OF THE QUEEN ■

IN 1601 THE EARL of Essex led an uprising against Queen Elizabeth. It failed and the handsome earl, once the queen's favourite, was beheaded. Among those who joined the uprising was Jack Wright, Guy Fawkes's old schoolfriend. He was reckoned England's finest swordsman. Another rebel was Robert Catesby, a wealthy landowner and now — after the death of his Protestant wife — a devout Catholic. Both men had hoped that Essex would change England's religious laws.

THE QUEEN DIES

Queen Elizabeth had not long to reign. In 1602 she was still fit enough to dance at court, but she was a sad, old woman, missing dead friends and without her old spark. She fell ill and on 24 March 1603 she died.

▲ The Earl of Essex, once the queen's favourite, was beheaded for treason.

▼ Up to months before her death, Elizabeth was 'frolicky and merry'. Here she enjoys dancing a gavotte.

~ JAMES I's FAMILY TREE ~

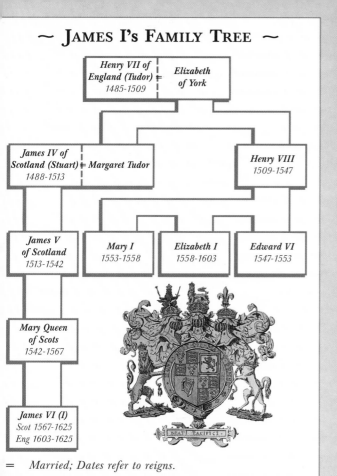

```
Henry VII of                    Elizabeth
England (Tudor) =               of York
1485-1509

   James IV of                              Henry VIII
Scotland (Stuart) = Margaret Tudor          1509-1547
   1488-1513

  James V                                                      
 of Scotland      Mary I         Elizabeth I      Edward VI
 1513-1542       1553-1558       1558-1603        1547-1553

Mary Queen
 of Scots
 1542-1567

 James VI (I)
Scot 1567-1625
Eng 1603-1625
```

= *Married; Dates refer to reigns.*

SCOTS IN ENGLAND

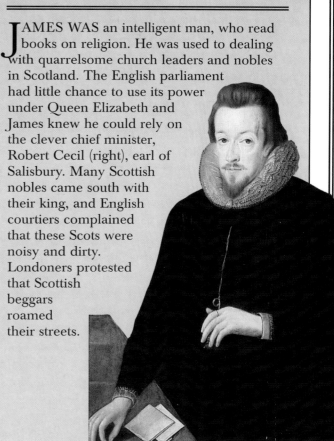

JAMES WAS an intelligent man, who read books on religion. He was used to dealing with quarrelsome church leaders and nobles in Scotland. The English parliament had little chance to use its power under Queen Elizabeth and James knew he could rely on the clever chief minister, Robert Cecil (right), earl of Salisbury. Many Scottish nobles came south with their king, and English courtiers complained that these Scots were noisy and dirty. Londoners protested that Scottish beggars roamed their streets.

At once, a courtier named Robert Carey rode north to Scotland and broke the news to England's new king, James VI of Scotland. Elizabeth had refused to name a successor. But the government agreed that James, the Protestant son of Mary Queen of Scots, was the man.

JAMES BECOMES KING

Hours after the queen died, her chief minister Robert Cecil read on London's streets the announcement that James was king. Bonfires were lit in celebration. People were sad at the death of the great queen. But it was almost 60 years since England had been ruled by an adult king, and that was Henry VIII. James was 36 and in good health. He and his Danish wife, Queen Anne, had two sons. It was a time of hope for a stable future.

PLAGUE AND RAIN

James was crowned in Westminster Abbey on 25 July. It poured with rain, sending people running for shelter. Plague had killed many people that summer, and the government feared that crowds might infect the lords and ladies. The stands built for ordinary Londoners stood half-finished and empty.

■ A SECRET MISSION ■

DURING 1603, GUY Fawkes went to Spain. He was sent by friends in the Netherlands to ask the Spanish king, Philip III, to help English Catholics. Guy Fawkes told the Spaniards that James was unfit to be king. The new Scottish king was (in Guy's words) a heretic, or false believer, who planned to make war on Catholic Europe. The Scots and English, he wrote, would never be friends and a Scottish king could never rule the two nations. All his life Guy Fawkes detested Scots!

EVENTS

1603 Guy Fawkes visits Philip III of Spain.
1604 James I opens parliament. He declares that the new habit of tobacco smoking is 'vile and stinking'. He orders a new translation of the Bible. Thomas Wintour visits Guy Fawkes in the Netherlands. Guy Fawkes travels to England.

A FRUITLESS MISSION

Guy returned empty-handed. Spain was not interested in plots. Two years before, Thomas Wintour had also been to Spain, seeking aid for English Catholics. He too had gone away disappointed because Spain wanted peace. Besides, the pope had warned that an invasion of England would lead to the deaths of many English Catholics. Guy went back to his soldiering. He now called himself Guido, perhaps to show that he had joined the cause of Spain.

WILD SCHEMES

In England there were plenty of wild schemes in the air. Weeks after James arrived in England, a small group of Catholics plotted to hold him prisoner until he agreed to change the anti-Catholic

Robert Catesby

Thomas Winter

▶ **Conspirators: Thomas Wintour (or Winter) and his cousin Robert Catesby, the leader of the plot. It was Wintour who persuaded Guy Fawkes to join the conspiracy.**

THE NEW BIBLE

THE FIRST complete Bibl in English was made by John Wycliffe in the 1380s. Before then, only Latin Bibles were used. During the Reformation, new English Bibles were made by William Tyndale and Miles Coverdale in the 1520s and 1530s. Englis Catholics in France translated the New Testament into Englis in 1582. In 1604, James I ordered scholars to prepare a new English Bible based on th earlier translations. This new version appeared in 1611 and known as the Authorized, or King James, Version.

laws. The plan was never put into action. Wiser Catholics heard of it and were horrified; Sir Thomas Tresham hurried to tell James that Catholics were loyal. The Spanish ambassador to England believed that English Catholics were 'in such a timid fear of one another' that they were not likely to rise up against their new king.

JAMES DISAPPOINTS CATHOLICS

In January 1604, the king and queen rode through the streets of London for the official opening of parliament. People cheered Prince Henry, a handsome ten-year-old, who bowed in return. James was pleased by his warm welcome. But to the dismay of English Catholics, James declared his belief that Catholics were 'superstitious'. There would be no change in the anti-Catholic laws.

A NEW PLOT

Early in 1604, Thomas Wintour went from England to visit Guy Fawkes in the Netherlands. His business was deadly

secret. He believed the new king, James, would never be a friend to the Catholics. He told Guy of a new plot.

In April 1604, Guy Fawkes returned to England with Wintour. The two soldiers moved warily, as if in enemy territory. Their mission was murder.

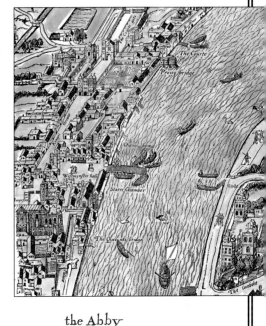

▶ A map of the time showing the position of Westminster Hall where the lords met – and where Guy Fawkes was later tried.

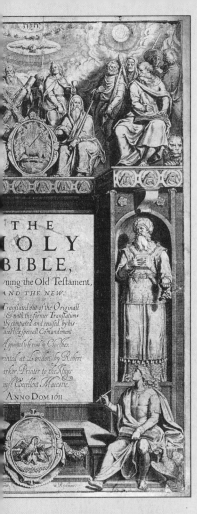

▲ The title page of the King James Version of the Bible, published in 1611.

◀ King James was a devout Protestant, with no time for Catholic or Puritan ideas.

▼ Westminster showing the Abbey, Hall and Parliament House, as they were in Guy Fawkes's day. Today's Houses of Parliament date from the 1800s.

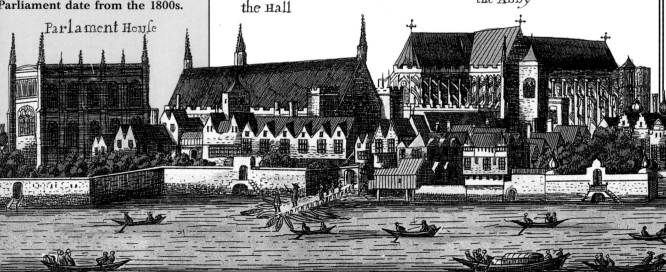

Parliament House

the Hall

the Abby

■ THE CONSPIRACY ■

THE LEADER OF the plot was Robert Catesby, Tom Wintour's cousin. Catesby had also joined the earl of Essex's rebellion and been heavily fined for it. He had friends among wealthy Catholics who sheltered priests. After his wife's death, he had become an ardent Catholic, convinced that he must do God's will.

On Sunday 20 May 1604, Catesby, Wintour, Fawkes, Jack Wright and Thomas Percy met at an inn called the Duck and Drake in London. It was time for action. Thomas Percy thumped his fist on the table, shouting 'Shall we always, gentlemen, talk and never do anything?' Catesby calmly told them his plan. They would blow up parliament with gunpowder, killing James and his advisers.

EVENTS

1604 Plotters begin storing gunpowder. The Constable of Castile, representing the king of Spain, visits James (August) to arrange a treaty between England and Spain. James orders the 'extermination' of Jesuits from England (September). Fines on Catholics are increased. Opening of parliament is postponed.

A DESPERATE REMEDY

On the day that he next opened parliament, the king and leading members of parliament would be together in one room. An explosion would kill all the enemies of Catholics in England. The plotters would then lead a Catholic rebellion. Princess Elizabeth, James's nine-year-old daughter who lived apart from her parents in the Midlands, would be made queen. She

▼ The house of the conspirators i Lambeth, just across the river from Westminster. Here Robert Keyes hid 36 barrels of gunpowder. Late under cover of darkness, he and Guy Fawkes ferried the barrels silently across the Thames.

MARTYRS ON BOTH SIDES

PROTESTANTS and Catholics in England could both claim martyrs, people who had died for their faith. In the reign of Mary I, the Protestant churchmen Latimer, Ridley and Cranmer had been found guilty of heresy and burned at the stake. In Elizabeth I's reign, Catholic priests such as the Jesuit Edmund Campion (left) were arrested, tortured and executed. The horrible punishment of hanging, drawing and quartering was common. The victim was hanged by the neck, taken down (often still alive), disembowelled and cut to pieces in front of the crowd.

Guy Fawkes with the 12 other conspirators. This imaginary scene shows them in a house near the Strand where they met to swear loyalty to one another and to make their secret plans.

would do as she was told and could be married to a Catholic prince. Spain would send help.

Guy and the others listened eagerly. Desperate times called for desperate remedies. The king's father, Lord Darnley, had been murdered in a gunpowder explosion when James was a baby. Now God would guide the plotters to get rid of James in the same way.

THE PLOT THICKENS . . .

In October, a sixth plotter, Robert Keyes, joined the group. He was to live in Catesby's London house, which was turned into a gunpowder store. Keyes's cousin was married to Ambrose Rookwood, a rich Catholic landowner with many horses. Horses would be vital when the rebellion started, so this was a useful contact. Catesby's servant Thomas Bates would carry messages.

. . . BUT IS DELAYED

Gunpowder was stacked ready when bad news came on Christmas Eve. Because

▲ James I's daughter, Elizabeth. The plotters planned to make her queen.

of the plague, parliament would not sit in February as planned. The king would not open the new parliament until October 1605. This gave the plotters more time to plan, but there was also a danger that their secret would slip out.

■ PLACING THE BOMB ■

EVEN IN 1604, London was a big, sprawling city. The Houses of Parliament, however, were not in the fine building we know as the Palace of Westminster today, which dates from the 1800s. The old palace where parliament then met was little more than a collection of houses grouped around Westminster Hall.

It was easy for the plotters to rent one of these houses, belonging to a man called John Whynniard. Like most city houses, it had a ground floor cellar for storing firewood and coal. Upstairs there was a small room, from which a door led

EVENTS

1605 Plotters supposedly stop digging the tunnel under parliament and rent the storehouse beneath the Lords' Chamber (March). Birth of James's daughter Mary (April), the first of his children to be born in England. William Shakespeare buys a house near his home town of Stratford-upon-Avon (July). A group of Catholics make a pilgrimage to the shrine of St Winifred at Holywell, in north Wales (August). The government later says this is part of the plot. An eclipse of the Sun is observed (October). Many people still believe such events signal great events.

THE MYSTERY OF THE TUNNEL

THE GOVERNMENT accused the plotters at their trial of trying to dig a tunnel under the Palace of Westminster. This work, begun in December 1604, was supposedly stopped in March when the ground proved too hard for digging. Whether the men did start such a tunnel is unclear. Guy Fawkes probably had enough experience. He had dug 'mines' in war. But the problems of digging a tunnel at Westminster would have been great. The government may have made up the story.

▶ An altarpiece in Gaywood Church, Norfolk, tells the story of the plot in pictures. The king and parliament are assembled, while the plotters carry out their dark deeds in the tunnel below. At the very top sits the God-like figure of King James in glory.

▲ Ferrying gunpowder across the Thames must have been difficult and dangerous.

directly into the House of Lords. The noble lords used such poky rooms to put on their furs and robes before meetings. There were no guards to check who came and went.

A NEW NAME

Like plotters in every age, Guy Fawkes took a false name. He became 'John Johnson' and moved into Whynniard's house to look after the gunpowder store. The number of plotters had grown when Robert Wintour, John Grant and Kit Wright joined in March. They met at inns, such as the Mermaid Tavern, where other diners and drinkers included soldiers, actors and the writers William Shakespeare and Ben Jonson. By the autumn, Ambrose Rookwood, Sir Everard Digby (a Midlands landowner who also owned horses) and Catesby's cousin Francis Tresham had also joined the gang, making 13 in all.

THE EXPLOSIVE

Gunpowder was bought and taken to Catesby's house in Lambeth on the south bank of the river Thames. Robert Keyes was in charge of moving it to Westminster. Thirty-six barrels were ferried across the river in a small boat and carried into the 'safe house'. By the end of July, the coal store had become a bomb. Guy had been chosen to carry out the most dangerous part of the plan. He was to light the fuse that would cause the gunpowder to explode and blow the House of Lords and King James to kingdom come.

◀ Sir Everard Digby, a handsome courtier who joined the conspirators.

▶ The playwright Ben Jonson may well have shared a drink with the conspirators – and spied on them.

■ DISCOVERY! ■

ON 4 NOVEMBER, the night air was cold and damp in the cellar beneath the House of Lords. Guy Fawkes shivered as he waited in the candlelight. All the gunpowder was in place. In just 12 hours, James I and his parliament would meet in the room above. Suddenly the candle flickered – the door opened. Seconds later, soldiers rushed in and seized him. Guy Fawkes did not fight back. With his hands tied, he was led away.

A MYSTERIOUS LETTER

Somebody had betrayed the plotters. On 26 October a letter had been delivered during the night to Lord Monteagle, a Catholic nobleman. The letter, unsigned, warned Monteagle to stay away from parliament on 5 November. It hinted at a 'terrible blow', but gave away nothing more.

THE PLOT IS UNCOVERED

Monteagle took the letter straight to Robert Cecil, the king's minister. He

EVENTS

1605 Lord Monteagle receives the letter warning him to stay away from the opening of parliament (26 October). He tells Robert Cecil. Guy Fawkes checks the gunpowder in the cellar (30 October). The plotters gather in London (31 October). The king is told of the letter (1 November). Catholics mark All Souls Day, the feast of the dead (2 November). Guy Fawkes waits, with a watch given to him by Keyes, to time the fuse that will set off the explosion (4 November). A first search by soldiers fails to find either him or the gunpowder. A second search is made in the middle of the night, and he is arrested.

GUNPOWDER

GUNPOWDER is an explosive mixture of saltpetre and sulphur. It was invented in China and first used in Europe during the Middle Ages. By the time of Guy Fawkes, it was used in guns, bombs and mines placed beneath enemy fortifications. The powder was made at powdermills and, after years of war, there was plenty in London, to be bought or stolen. However, when Guy Fawkes's gunpowder was removed from the cellar two days after his arrest, it was found to be 'decayed'. It had been stored too long. Even had he lit the fuse and made his getaway, it may not have exploded!

▼ **Eight of the thirteen plotters are shown in this engraving. Missing are Digby, Grant, Keyes, Rookwood and Tresham. The 'hatless' Thomas Bate was Catesby's servant. Catesby, Percy and the Wright brothers died while trying to escape arrest. The others were executed.**

Robert Winter · Christopher Wright · Iohn Wright · Thomas Percy · Guido Fawkes · Robert Catesby · Thomas Winter

waited – and why, no one knows for certain – until 1 November before showing it to the king. The king had returned to London after a hunting holiday.

James took the letter seriously. His father had, after all, been killed in a gunpowder explosion. A search of Westminster was ordered at once, but strangely the soldiers found nothing. It is possible that the searchers actually saw Guy Fawkes but went away, assuming that he was a servant with a large pile of what they thought was firewood.

Guy Fawkes laying the trail of gunpowder that was never lit.

▲ The lantern Guy Fawkes used to light his dark deed.

The king told Cecil to order a second search. Around midnight on 4 November, the soldiers went back. In the cellar below the Lords' Chamber, they found 'a very tall and desperate fellow', Guy Fawkes, waiting calmly with the barrels of gunpowder.

▼ At dead of night, guards caught Guy Fawkes hiding by the gunpowder.

* my lord out of the loue i beare ~~vnto~~ To some of youere freindz i haue a caer of youer preseruacion therfor i wousd... aduyse yowe as yowe tender youer lyf to deuys... some epscuse to shift of youer attendance at this parleament for god aud man hathe concurred to punishe the wickednes of this tyme and thinke not slightly e of this aduertisment but retiere youre self into youre countri whyeare youe... maye expect the euent in safti for thowghe theare be no apparance of anai stir yet i saye they shall receyue a terrible blowe this parleament and yet they shall not seie who hurts them this counsel is not to be contemned becauss it maye do youe good and can do youe no harme for the dangere is passed as soone as youe haue burnt the letter and i hope god wille gine yowe the grace to mak good use of it to whose holy protecction icoumend youe*

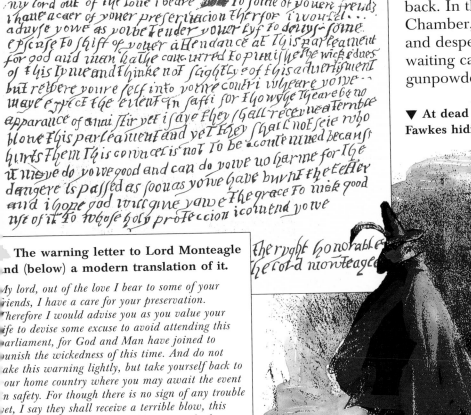

The warning letter to Lord Monteagle and (below) a modern translation of it.

the ryght honorable the lord mouteagle

My lord, out of the love I bear to some of your friends, I have a care for your preservation. Therefore I would advise you as you value your life to devise some excuse to avoid attending this parliament, for God and Man have joined to punish the wickedness of this time. And do not take this warning lightly, but take yourself back to your home country where you may await the event in safety. For though there is no sign of any trouble yet, I say they shall receive a terrible blow, this parliament, and yet they shall not see who hurts them. This counsel is not to be dismissed because it may do you good and can do you no harm, for the danger is passed as soon as you have burned this letter. And I hope God will give you the grace to make good use of it, to whose holy protection I commend you.

To the right honourable The Lord Monteagle

■ CAPTURE AND DEATH ■

SOME TIME AFTER midnight on 4 November 1605, Guy Fawkes was dragged into the king's chamber for questioning. He refused to give his name and was bundled away by soldiers to the Tower of London. He remained defiant, refusing to name the other plotters.

After two days of questioning, all he confessed was that he might be a Catholic. King James ordered that the strongest methods (torture) be used to force the silent soldier to confess.

THE CONFESSION

At last, Guy admitted that his name was Fawkes, not Johnson. Gasp by gasp, the torturers dragged from his lips the details of the plot. By this time, Guy Fawkes was a broken man, barely able to sign his name on his confession.

THE PLOTTERS MEET THEIR FATE

Catesby and the other plotters had fled to the Midlands. Three days after Guy's arrest, they were hiding at Holbeach House in Worcestershire. Their gunpowder was wet from drenching rain and they foolishly tried to dry it before an open fire. There was an explosion which blinded John Grant.

PRISONER ON THE RAC[K]

TORTURE was used to ma[ke] a prisoner talk. First came the manacles, iron bands arou[nd] the wrists and fastened by chai[n] to the wall. The prisoner dangled, painfully, and his han[ds] could be maimed for ever. If a prisoner still kept silent, he wa[s] placed on the rack (right). Spreadeagled, his arms and leg[s] were held by ropes wound around wheels. Turning the wheels tightened the ropes. No[w] even the strongest man could stand the rack for long.

▼ **A transcript of part of Guy Fawkes's confession (right).**

Concerning Duke Charles, the king's second son, we had sundry consultations how to seize on his person, but because we found no means how to compass it (the Duke being kept near London) where we had not forces enough, we resolved to serve ourselves with the Lady Elizabeth.

The names of other principal persons that were made privy afterwards to this horrible conspiracy.
Everard Digby, Knight   (signed) Guido Fawk[es]
Ambrose Rookwood
Francis Tresham
John Grant
Robert ~~Keyes~~ Wynter

(Witnessed) Edward Coke (Attorney-General) W[illiam]
Waad (Lieutenant of the Tower of London)

▼ **Guy Fawkes was dragged before the king. He refused to give his name or to identify the other plotters.**

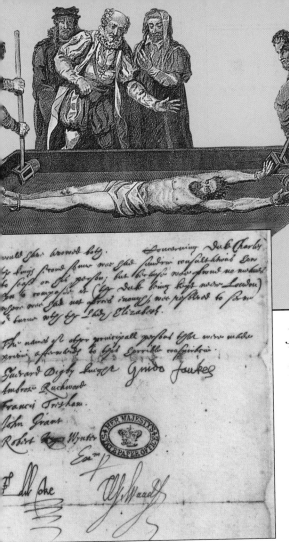

Two hundred soldiers surrounded the house. With swords drawn, the desperate plotters met their fate. Catesby and Percy were shot dead by the same bullet. The Wright brothers were also killed. The rest were taken prisoner and brought for trial to London, where Francis Tresham died.

THE TRIAL

The Gunpowder Plot trial was held in Westminster Hall. It lasted only hours. On 27 January 1606, Guy Fawkes and the seven other conspirators left alive were sentenced to a traitor's death – to be hanged, drawn and quartered.

The executions took place on 30 and 31 January. Soldiers lined the streets as Robert Wintour, Sir Everard Digby, John Grant and Thomas Bates were dragged on sledge-like wooden hurdles to the scaffold. Guy Fawkes, Tom Wintour, Ambrose Rookwood and Robert Keyes died the next day.

Guy Fawkes, the 'great devil of all', was last on to the scaffold. He was so weak that he had to be helped up the steps by the hangman but was strong enough to mutter a prayer. Unlike some of his friends, he died at once and so was spared further pain.

▼ The execution of the gunpowder plotters.

■ THE END ■

THE HEADS OF the traitors were placed on spiked poles as 'prey to the fowls of the air'. They were a grim warning to any other plotters who might dare to threaten the king or his government.

On the night of 5 November 1605, people in London celebrated the news that the Gunpowder Plot had been foiled. They lit bonfires in the street. Some in the crowd had probably seen people burned at the stake. So it was no surprise if someone made a dummy of Guy Fawkes and burned it as part of the celebrations.

CATHOLICS ARRESTED

The government accused a Catholic priest named Father Henry Garnet of being the brains behind the plot. He was arrested and executed on 3 May 1606. Father Garnet had known Catesby and had heard whispers of a plot, but there was no proof that he had helped to plan it.

The plotters' relatives and friends were all under suspicion. Many

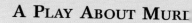

A PLAY ABOUT MURI

IN 1606, *Macbeth*, the latest play by William Shakespea was performed before the kin and queen. It was a shocking story, of treason, plotting and murder of a king of Scotland. was surely no coincidence tha Shakespeare had chosen such

▲ Father Henry Garnet, accused of masterminding the plot.

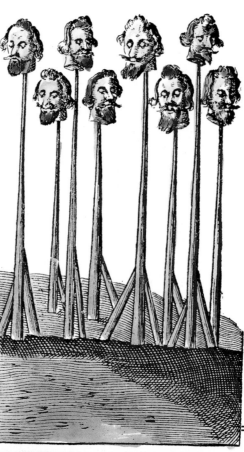

▶ The plotters' heads were placed on spikes as a warning to others.

for his latest play. James, the [s]ottish king who had so luckily [esc]aped murder, no doubt [app]lauded loudest of all at the [en]d.

'Ring the alarum-bell! Murder [an]d treason' – the alarm scene in [1]901 production of [Sh]akespeare's *Macbeth*.

Catholics feared arrest. Catholic women who had sheltered priests were questioned. Catholic priests in hiding feared for their lives. Father John Gerard, another friend of Catesby, escaped by ship to France, disguised as a servant. Pamphlets blamed the pope for the plot, and stirred up bad feeling between Protestants and Catholics in England.

MYSTERY AND MURDER FEARS

Mystery still surrounds the Gunpowder Plot. Some historians believe the government knew about it early on, from its spies. If so, the Monteagle letter (now in the Public Record Office in London) may not have been written by one of the plotters at all.

Whatever the truth, James was saved from being blown up. He still believed he might be murdered and wore extra-padded clothes for protection against a knife-thrust. In his age, death by dagger or sword-thrust was more common than by gunpowder.

▶ Foreign interest: a Dutch illustration of the plot and (below) a German drawing of the horror that might have been.

■ GUY FAWKES REMEMBERED ■

IF THE GUNPOWDER Plot had succeeded, would England have become a Catholic country again? No one can say. The plot made the government even more suspicious of people who did not follow the 'official' line in religion. Laws against Catholics became more strict. Catholics could not be lawyers, army or navy officers, or members of parliament. The last anti-Catholic laws were not ended until 1829. Strict Protestants such as Puritans were also treated harshly, which is why the Pilgrim Fathers set sail for the New World in 1620.

EVENTS

1611 *New wave of Scots and English settlement in Ireland begins, the 'Plantation of Ulster'.*
1612 *Death of Prince Henry, aged 18, from typhoid.*
1613 *A new law to make all Catholics wear red hats is turned down in parliament.*
1620 *Pilgrim Fathers sail to America in the* Mayflower.
1625 *Death of James I, who is succeeded by his second son, Charles I.*

PLOTS EVERYWHERE

For years, Catholics were blamed for every 'plot' against the government or king. Today, Yeomen of the Guard still search the Houses of Parliament on the night before the monarch opens parliament. More serious measures are also taken against modern terrorism, not only at Westminster, but in government buildings around the world. Blowing up buildings was rare in Guy Fawkes's time. Today, sadly, terrorist bombs are more common.

THE HOUSES OF PARLIAMENT

THE PALACE of Westminster was a royal residence in the 900s, when Edward the Confessor built th first palace. In 1512 the buildings were damaged by fi and Henry VIII moved house to St James's Palace. In 1547 Edward VI gave the chapel of

▼ **Puritans leaving for America to seek freedom of worship.**

the old palace to the House of Commons as a meeting place. This building was destroyed by fire in 1834. The new Houses of Parliament were open by 1852, and – though damaged by bombs in World War II – continue to be the seat of parliament to this day.

The state opening of parliament is a grand occasion. Security is tighter now than it was in Guy Fawkes's day.

◀ Yeomen of the Guard search the cellars of the Houses of Parliament before the state opening of parliament but the ceremony is not open to the public. Yeomen Warders, who wear similar uniforms, can be seen at the Tower of London.

▼ Effigies of Guy Fawkes were once carried through the streets and burned on bonfires as an expression of horror. Today Bonfire Night is an excuse for fireworks.

BONFIRE NIGHT

Guy Fawkes Night, or Bonfire Night, became a popular celebration in England. It was the only national holiday allowed under Oliver Cromwell's Commonwealth. It crossed the Atlantic, where in 1780 American colonists burned 'guys' of Britain's prime minister, Lord North.

In Britain, Guy Fawkes is remembered every year on 5 November. Stuffed guys of the gunpowder plotter are wheeled through the streets, their makers collecting 'pennies for the guy' to give them money for fireworks. The guys are set on top of bonfires and burned amid the scream of rockets and cascades of coloured sparks. Guy Fawkes has become a legend – and an excuse to let off fireworks, burn rubbish and make lots of noise!

■ GLOSSARY ■

AMBASSADOR Representative of one country sent to another, to conduct government business.

ANONYMOUS LETTER A letter not signed by the person writing it.

ARMADA An invasion fleet; Spain sent the great armada of 1588 to attack England.

BELIEFS Ideas that people think are true.

CATHOLIC A follower of the Christian faith who obeys the teachings of the Roman Catholic Church and its head, the pope.

COLONISTS People who settle in a new land, or colony, which is usually governed by their own country.

COMMONWEALTH Name given to the period after the execution of King Charles I when Britain was ruled by Oliver Cromwell and parliament.

CONFESSION Admitting the truth.

CONSPIRATOR A person who takes part in a conspiracy, or plot.

EFFIGY Lifelike model of a person.

FUSE Length of string or wood that burns slowly when lit. Fuses were used to set off gunpowder.

GUNPOWDER An explosive made from charcoal, saltpetre (potassium nitrate) and sulphur.

GUY Dummy figure, named after Guy Fawkes, that is stuffed with straw, paper or rags, and traditionally burnt on bonfires on 5 November in Britain.

HERETIC Person who holds views opposed to the teachings of the official church or other religion.

INTERROGATION Questioning, usually of a prisoner to find out what he or she knows.

JESUIT Member of a Catholic religious order called the Society of Jesus, founded by Ignatius Loyola in 1534.

LATIN Language of the ancient Romans, used by the Roman Catholic Church in Guy Fawkes's day, as well as for official documents and scholarly books.

MARTYR A person who is prepared to die rather than give up strongly held beliefs.

MINE In warfare in the 1500s and 1600s, a tunnel dug beneath a fortification and filled with gunpowder. When the gunpowder exploded, the wall above collapsed.

NETHERLANDS See **SPANISH NETHERLANDS**

NEW WORLD Name given to North and South America after their discovery by Europeans in the late 1400s.

PERSECUTION Unfair or cruel treatment of people.

PLAGUE Outbreak of a disease, particularly bubonic plague, which was highly infectious and almost always fatal.

POWDERMILL Workshop where gunpowder was made by grinding and mixing the chemicals.

PROTESTANTS Christians who belong to churches outside the Roman Catholic or Eastern Orthodox churches.

RACK Instrument of torture once used in prisons to make people confess.

RECUSANT Person, especially a Roman Catholic, who refused to attend the Church of England during the time when this was compulsory.

REFORMATION Religious reform movement begun by Martin Luther in Germany in the 1500s, which led to the emergence of Protestant churches.

SAPPER Name given to a soldier who dug tunnels for explosive mines under enemy fortifications.

SCAFFOLD Wooden platform on which people were hanged or beheaded.

SPANISH NETHERLANDS The lands known as the Low Countries, today Belgium and Holland.

STRAND, THE An old London street that runs by the Thames.

SULPHUR Yellowish element that burns easily and gives off a choking gas.

TOLERANCE Believing that all people – of all religious faiths or none – should be treated alike and fairly.

TORTURE Inflicting pain on people to punish them or to make them say or do what the torturer wants.

WESTMINSTER Area of central London alongside the Thames where Britain's government buildings stand.

YEOMAN OF THE GUARD The monarch's personal bodyguard whose duties nowadays are largely ceremonial. Yeomen warders, who wear similar Tudor uniforms, work at the Tower of London.

PLACES TO VISIT

Palace of Westminster,
London.
You can queue up to enter the House of Commons and the House of Lords when parliament is in session. To see other areas, you must apply to a Member of Parliament.

York
Guy Fawkes's birthplace and school.

Public Record Office,
London.
You can arrange to see Guy Fawkes's confession and other documents.

Tower of London
Where Guy Fawkes was imprisoned and executed.

Museum of London
Background information about the time when Guy Fawkes lived.

Lewes or Rye,
Sussex.
For Bonfire Night celebrations.

PRIEST HOLES
You can see priest holes at the following National Trust properties:

Baddesley Clinton Hall,
Solihull, Warwickshire.

Coughton Court,
Warwickshire.

Moseley Old Hall,
Staffordshire.

Oxburgh Hall,
Norfolk.

Scotney Castle,
Kent.